Keeping Parents Posted

Information about children's schooling and other educational matters

Prepared by
**Frances Allen,
Graham Atherton**
and
Nick Doyle

Scottish Consumer Council,
in association with the National Consumer
Council and the Welsh Consumer Council.

Edinburgh
Her Majesty's Stationery Office

Scottish Consumer Council
314 St Vincent Street
Glasgow G3 8XW

© Crown Copyright 1988
First published 1988

Illustrations by 'Larry'

ISBN 0 11 493424 X

Contents

Parents need written information in order to make sensible decisions about their children's schooling and to reach sound judgements about the way educational services are run. This is recognised increasingly by all of those involved in education — teachers, officials and politicians — as well as by parents themselves.

Recent years have brought parents and other members of the public new rights to receive or see copies of booklets, reports and other documents issued by local authorities. The Education Act 1980, for England and Wales, and the Education (Scotland) Act 1981, for example, entitle parents to written information about schools. The Education (No. 2) Act 1986 obliges school governors in England and Wales to publish and distribute to parents an annual report on their work. The Local Government (Access to Information) Act 1985 allows the public to see reports of meetings of their local council. These rights are extended in very recent changes in the law proposed at the time of going to press.

This publication signposts parents and parents' representatives (on school boards, governing bodies, parents' and parent-teacher associations) to various official and semi-official sources of written information now available about schooling and other educational matters. Such information could be of importance to parents when deciding which school they would send their child to, discussing their child's schoolwork, considering what specialist help their child might need, responding to plans to close down a school and a range of other situations covered in this booklet.

The publication will be particularly useful to individual parents of children about to start school or already at school. It will also be of interest to school staff, school board members, governing bodies, elected representatives and others whose work brings them into contact with parents. I commend it to you.

Barbara Kelly
Chairman
Scottish Consumer Council

K.E.

The SCC would like to thank staff from the following organisations for their help and encouragement in commenting on the draft of this guide:

Convention of Scottish Local Authorities
Grampian Regional Council
Lothian Regional Council
Scottish Education Department
Scottish Parent Teacher Council.

We are also grateful to the following individuals for their comments: Julie Collis (Scottish Parent Teacher Council), Tina Day (National Consumer Council), Maurice Frankel (Campaign for Freedom of Information), Dr Derek Manson-Smith (Freedom of Information Consultant), and Elizabeth Wallis (Advisory Centre for Education). Richard Cox (Department of Celtic Studies, Glasgow University) translated the text (on pages 82-3) into Gaelic and Beti Wynn Thomas (National Consumer Council) translated the text (on page 85) into Welsh.

Members of the SCC Education Committee: Father Matt McManus (Chairman), Pat Bolton, Deirdre Hutton, Helen Millar and Sylvia Sandeman.

Parents are legally responsible for their child's education and welfare. They have not only a right but a duty to see that their child is properly educated. This means parents being informed as much as possible about educational services on offer. It is also in the interest of the child to have well-informed parents, whose attitudes, research has shown, are related to how well children do at school.

A regular flow of information between parents and their children's school and the education authority also counteracts confusion, misunderstandings and suspicion. It raises the level of parents' interest in and support for their children's education. It saves school staff and officials' time if they do not have to repeat the same information and explanations endlessly to a succession of parents. And it helps councils to explain their objectives and policies.

Written information is invaluable if you cannot get to your child's school or to the council offices easily. But it is also useful even if you do manage to see teachers or attend parents' meetings: it gives you ideas about what you should be looking for, the questions you should be asking teachers and officials, improvements that you should be seeking for your children's school or for education services generally.

This publication tells you what sorts of information are available; what the various reports, brochures and papers look like and contain; how to get hold of them (and whether you have a right to demand them); some hints on how to read them and what importance to place on the information; and, finally, some ideas on how to put this information to good use.

Part One is a guide to the different types of information:

Section 1   *Information about your child* deals with information specifically about your child and his or her school.

Section 2   *Information about a school* deals with information you can get about a particular school.

Section 3   *Information from an education authority (Scotland) or local education authority (England and Wales)* deals with information about the educational policies and practices of your regional or islands council (Scotland) or county or borough council (England and Wales).

Section 4 *Information from central government* deals with information on education policy and ideas generally and how these are put into practice through laws and regulations.

Part Two of this guide gives examples of how this information can be *used* by parents either in connection with their own children's education (Section 5) or in dealing with general educational matters (Section 6).

▷ Publications giving more detailed information about many of the topics covered by this publication are listed at the end. Particularly useful are **for Scotland** — the Scottish Consumer Council's *The Law of the School* (HMSO Books, 1987), and **for England and Wales** — the *ACE Guide to Education Law*, the *ACE Summary of the Education (No. 2) Act 1986* and the *ACE Special Education Handbook*.

At the time of writing two new education bills, one for Scotland, the other for England and Wales, were being considered by parliament. Expected changes in the law are mentioned where relevant in the text, but readers should check with an advice centre or solicitor for further information.

The Scottish, National and Welsh Consumer Councils regret that they cannot deal with individual problems or enquiries about topics discussed in this or other publications.

Part One: What information is available

1 Information about your child

Talking to your child as often as possible — and looking at work brought home from school — is an important way of finding out about how well he or she is doing at school. You should be on the alert for any difficulties before they blow up into big crises. Do not hesitate to inform the school of any problems your child is having; staff may be able to provide support or guidance of their own in many cases.

It is easier to find out about your child's schooling if you are already in regular touch with the school. If you go to parents' meetings and other functions in the school, you will get to know your child's teachers better. Teachers will see that you take an interest in your child's schooling and should therefore do their best to inform you about how your child is getting on.

If the school does not have parents' meetings, or if these do not happen often, arrange to speak to a member of the school staff yourself. Telephone the school for an appointment. You can contact the school as often as you need to; however busy the school might be, you should expect school staff to be ready to listen to your concerns.

Approaching the school

Nursery and primary schools will often go out of their way to make parents feel welcome at school. You may be encouraged to call in and see your child's class teacher or the headteacher. You may be allowed to see classes at work.

When your child reaches secondary school, the links are likely to be more formal. Often it is difficult to know whom to contact, particularly as your child may not have a single class teacher. There is usually a senior staff member, such as an assistant headteacher, responsible for your child's year at school. In Scotland, specialist teachers of guidance should also be available to give personal, curricular or careers guidance.

Contacting other parents

If your child is having difficulties which are shared by other children, for example too many distractions or interruptions in class, consider contacting other parents to discuss what can be done. You could also raise any problems with your parents' representative on the school board or governing body or with your school's parents' or parent-teacher association (if there is one).

Approaching the education authority

If you are discouraged from visiting the school or speaking to staff without good cause, you should complain to the education authority (see under "Approaching the Education Authority" on page 53 for guidance about doing this).

You will usually be sent a report on your child's progress at school at least once a year. Insist on a report being sent to you if this has not been done. The education authority normally decides what sorts of information school reports should contain.

Reports will usually cover:

- **progress in school work**
  Sometimes there is a box for each teacher to make individual comments; sometimes the school makes only general remarks, such as 'satisfactory', 'poor' and so on. If exams have been taken, there may be a summary of the marks given.

- **behaviour**
  The report should include comments on your child's attitude to work, behaviour in class and in the school generally.

- **attendance**
  The report will include a record of your child's attendance.

How are school reports issued?

The school report is intended to be read by both you and your child; it is normally given to your child to bring home. The school's handbook should give details about how and where school reports are issued. Often schools provide a slip for you to return saying you have received the report and may also leave a space for your own comments.

Making use of school reports

The school report provides an important starting point for you to discuss your child's progress with school staff, regardless of how well or badly your child is doing.

Fortunately school reports rarely contain comments such as "Regrettably he is doing his best …", but you may find that you have to read between the lines to understand what a report is saying. The report on its own may not convey much that you do not know already or it may not give enough detailed information about your child's difficulties. You should therefore not hesitate to speak to school staff about anything in the report you do not understand or which is unclear.

You can normally speak to school staff at any time of the school year to discuss your child's progress, and schools will often make special arrangements of their own at least once a year for you to do so. Reports on children's progress should normally be made available to custodial and non-custodial parents, if living apart, as should arrangements for meeting staff, but you should check on the particular practices of the school or education authority about this.

At the time of writing, the government announced plans to make school reports on a child's achievements clearer and more comprehensive for parents.

What is a school record for?

In Scotland the school must keep a progress record on your child. In England and Wales there is as yet no legal obligation to do so, but the school will certainly have a record on your child and will follow guidelines on style and content issued by your education authority.

The school collects this information to use in connection with your child's progress at school. It is used by staff in helping your child to choose the right courses and subjects, for example.

What sorts of information do records contain?

- a pupil's full name and address, date of birth, position in the family, a parent's name and address, occupation, and where appropriate, place of work
- the name and address of an emergency contact
- the schools attended by the pupil (including independent schools) with the dates of admission and leaving and the name of the class left
- the results, with dates, of any psychological or aptitude tests given to the pupil
- a note of any reason why the pupil may have learning difficulties
- the pupil's health record
- information where appropriate about relationships with fellow pupils or teachers, attitudes and behaviour
- dates and details of any exclusions from school, including any appeal committee or, in Scotland, sheriff court decisions
- the pupil's yearly educational progress
- for secondary school pupils, information about any positions of responsibility held, such as school prefect.

Can parents see the school record?

Parents do not (at the time of writing) have any automatic right to see school progress records on their child. An *Access to Personal Files Act* passed in 1987 would have entitled parents to do so, but the part dealing with educational records was later dropped during the bill's passage through parliament, on the understanding that the government already had power to allow the right of access.*

In Scotland

Your education authority may in any case agree to let you see your child's progress record, and it may be possible for you to have the record corrected or brought up-to-date (or for your comments on a disputed part of the record to be inserted or attached). You may not necessarily be shown any or all parts of the record if the well-being of the child might be badly affected. And it appears at present that access, if granted, applies to the parents, not to the child.

In England and Wales

A few authorities have adopted policies giving parents access to records, though, as in Scotland, there are restrictions on what you will be allowed to see. Some of these authorities give pupils aged 16 or over the same rights as parents.

*At the time of writing, the government announced that it intended to introduce legislation for England and Wales (which could extend to Scotland) giving parents access to school files or records on their child.

Who else can see the record?

In Scotland

The school record may not be shown to social workers, the police or prospective employers if there are no educational grounds for doing so, although it may be referred to when writing references for your child. Details about any exclusions from school which have been appealed against successfully may not be revealed to outsiders at all.

In England and Wales

Policies on who may see school records vary from authority to authority. Some authorities leave it entirely to the discretion of the headteacher.

What can you do with this information?

Your child's school record could give a useful insight into what the school thinks of your child and any problems he or she may have.

It would certainly give more information than the much shorter and more formal school report that you already receive. So it may be well worth your asking to see your child's records.

The school or the education authority may agree to let you see them even if it is not required to by law. If it refuses, ask the education authority for its policy on parents' access to educational records. If it does not plan to make these records accessible, then as a member of a parent teacher association, school board or governing body, press your education authority to change its position.

Computerised school records

You have the right to see any records on your child which are intended for use on a computer. These records — which include printed papers — could be at the school or in the education authority offices. The sort of information that may be computerised is exam results or other qualifications. These need not be shown to you if they are intended only for research or statistical purposes. Ask the education authority or school what computer records are kept on your child. You can then ask to inspect and if necessary correct these.

Recording of special educational needs

Children are said to have special educational needs if:

- they have significantly greater difficulty in learning than the majority of other children of their age

- they have disabilities which prevent or hinder them from making use of educational facilities normally provided for children of their age.

The education authority is responsible for finding out whether your child has special educational needs and, if so, how to cater for them. The first stage is a lengthy assessment process, when you should be given chances to give your views and to ask questions. Then, if the education authority thinks your child's difficulties are serious ones, it is likely to open a special file, called a Record of Needs. This describes your child's difficulties, and what additional or special help is needed for his or her education. The education authority must carefully consider your views before finalising the Record.

What information does the Record contain?

- you and your child's name and address

- the address of the 'Named Person' (if you elect to have one). This is the person the education authority appoints to advise and help you. You should expect this to be somebody you can trust or rely upon, such as a professional worker or friend

- a description of your child's health, interests, ability, emotional development and so on

- a description of any learning difficulties, disabilities or problems your child has

- a statement of what your child requires, for example, special teaching or care

- information on what the authority proposes to do (this is one part of the record you *cannot* appeal against)

- the school to be attended

- any views that you as parent or guardian of the child have expressed, including your views about what the authority proposes to do

- information about any reviews or reassessment of your child's special education needs that have been carried out since the original assessment

- a list of people who have seen the Record of Needs.

Changes may be made to the entries in these parts of the Record as a result of your child's special needs coming under formal review.

Who sees the record?

The education authority keeps the final version of the Record of Needs but must give you a copy. There may also be a copy kept at your child's school. It may also be seen by:

- teachers, psychologists, medical staff and social workers dealing with your child

- the Named Person

- the official dealing with your case if you appeal against the Record

- the reporter to the children's panel, should your child be referred to a children's hearing

- people engaged in educational, medical or social research (but the child's name may not normally be shown)

- any other person approved by the education authority.

The Record of Needs is a very important source of information for the parents of a child with special education needs. But you will also need other information, as well as lots of advice and explanations of how your child can be educated. For this reason it is essential that you have close contact with the education authority and in particular that you use the Named Person to help you get all the information you want.

A Record of Needs ends if an appeal or review decides to discontinue it, if your child is leaving school, if your child has reached school leaving age and asks for it to be ended, or if your child has reached 18.

How much say do you have over what goes in the Record?

When the education authority is preparing a Record of Needs, it will send a draft of the Record to you so that you can tell it if there is anything which you think is wrong or has been left out. Your replies will be added to the folder and form part of the record. You will then be given a copy of the Record of Needs. Any time there is additional information, for example a review of your child's special needs, this will be added to both the education authority's and your copies of the record.

You can appeal against a decision to open a Record for your child, against certain parts of the Record or against certain changes to the Record (after review). You can also now appeal against a decision *not* to record your child. When the education authority gives you your copy of the Record of Needs, it will tell you how to appeal.

➪ For more information see *Special Educational Needs,* a free booklet produced by the Scottish Education Department, available from the Scottish Information Office, your education authority or your local Citizens Advice Bureau. *The Law of the School* also includes a detailed section on "Special Educational Needs".

What is a Statement of Special Educational Needs?

In England and Wales children are said to have "special educational needs" if they need additional or different educational provision for a learning difficulty.

If the local education authority thinks that your child has special educational needs, it has to make an assessment of them and, if necessary, make a Statement of Special Educational Needs. You will be given the chance to make your views known during the assessment and to appeal against the educational provision specified in the Statement.

What sort of information does it contain?

- you and your child's name and address

- the education authority's view of your child's special educational needs

- the special educational provision the authority thinks appropriate to meet those needs — for example, the facilities and equipment, staffing arrangements and curriculum

- the type of school that the authority thinks appropriate and the name of a particular school if it has one in mind

- details of any education otherwise than at school

- any additional non-educational provision to be made by either the education, health or social services authorities

- all the representations, evidence and advice taken into account by the authority in making the Statement. This includes: parental representations and advice, educational, medical and psychological advice, any advice from other sources, and any information supplied by the district health authority or social services authority.

Changes may be made in the Statement following annual reviews.

The local education authority keeps the final version of the Statement but must give you a copy and tell you of your right of appeal against the special educational provision specified in it, and give you the name of the person to contact for information and advice about your child's special educational needs. The authority cannot show the Statement to anyone without your consent, unless it thinks that disclosure is in your child's interests. So it could be seen by:

- teachers, psychologists, medical staff and social workers dealing with your child
- officers of the authority.

It may also be seen:

- by people involved in an appeal if you object to the education provision specified in the Statement
- on the order of the courts or for the purposes of criminal proceedings
- for purposes of investigation by the local ombudsman
- by educational researchers, provided nothing published identifies you or your child, and the research is likely to advance the education of children with special educational needs.

The Statement of Special Educational Needs applies until your child's nineteenth birthday. The education authority can propose to stop maintaining it after a review. The Statement will also cease if you are successful in appealing against it.

You have the right to be involved in the assessment procedure:

- you have the right to comment on the notice from the authority that it proposes to assess your child
- you have the right to be present at examinations and to submit information
- you can make representations on the draft Statement and ask for meetings with the authority's professionals
- you can appeal against the statement, first to a local appeal committee, and, if unsuccessful, to the Secretary of State for Education and Science (in Wales, to the Secretary of State for Wales).

⟳ For more information, see the Advisory Centre for Education's *Special Education Handbook*.

Types of information available

The last section discussed how you could find out more information about the schooling of *your child*. This section tells you what you can find out about a *particular school*. It deals with the following types of information:

- school information — information about a particular school
  (To find out what schools there are near you, what areas they cover and what is the policy on admissions to these schools, see Section 3.)

- information on a school's examination results

- in England and Wales, governors' annual reports for parents

- in England and Wales, the governors' statement of the school's curricular aims and information about school syllabuses and other educational matters*

- H.M. Inspectors' reports

- newsletters and other information produced by the school.

*There will be regulations on the content of these policy statements, of information about syllabuses and of additional information following legislation on the national curriculum, which was being considered by parliament at the time of writing.

In Scotland:

An education authority is bound by law to provide three types of information about schools in its area. These are *basic* information, *school* information, and *supplementary* information. Basic information and supplementary information do not apply to just one school and are therefore discussed under "Information about education in your area" on pages 41 to 53.

In England and Wales:

Local education authorities have to provide two types of information. These are general information and detailed information about individual fully maintained, that is, 'county' schools. General information is discussed on pages 47 to 49. The same requirements apply to the two main types of voluntary school: the governors of aided and special agreement schools are responsible for publishing the information, although they can ask the education authority to publish it on their behalf. (The authority is responsible for producing information about controlled schools.) Voluntary school governors are also responsible for producing information about their school's admission policies and arrangements (though, again, the authority may do it on their behalf). This information is the same as for the authority's own fully maintained schools — see under "Admission arrangements" on page 47 for details.

What does school information cover?

The information which must be issued about each school covers:

- **Factual information about the school**

  In Scotland:

  — the school's name, address, telephone number

  — the name of the headteacher and the number of staff, including the specialist responsibilities of staff in special schools

  — the number and sex of pupils normally admitted

  — the school's denominational status (if any)

  — normal starting and dismissal times

— organisation of the school day

— term times and holiday dates

— schools to which pupils will normally transfer, for example, after leaving primary school

— special needs catered for, if the school is a special school.

In England and Wales

— the school's name, address, telephone number

— the name of the headteacher and of the chair of the school's governors

— type of school, that is, whether it is a county, voluntary school or a special school; a primary, middle or secondary school or a sixth form college; a comprehensive, secondary modern, grammar or bilateral school; a coeducational or single sex school; a day or boarding school or both

— the school's denominational status (if any).

- **The school's educational practices**

In Scotland:

— the school's educational aims

— arrangements for parents to visit the school, for example, to discuss their child's progress

— what is taught (curriculum) at different age levels and, in the case of secondary schools, school subject options and choices available and arrangements for consulting parents about these

— arrangements for assessing pupils' progress and reporting this to parents

— in the case of secondary schools, whether pupils are grouped through 'streaming' or 'setting' or by 'mixed ability'

— provision of religious education and observance, including arrangements for educating pupils of parents who have exercised their right to withdraw their child from this

— provision of personal, curricular and careers guidance (secondary schools)

— out of school activities (clubs, sports, etc)

— facilities at the school for sports and outdoor activities.

In England and Wales:

— what is taught (curriculum) at different age levels, the subject options available and how parents and pupils make choices between subjects, and the level up to which subjects are taught

— how sex education is taught

— what careers education is provided

— how teaching is organised, particularly whether pupils are grouped by 'streaming', 'setting' or by 'mixed ability'

— provision of religious education, including arrangements for educating pupils of parents who have exercised their right to withdraw their child from this or from religious worship

— provision of pastoral care and, in secondary schools, careers guidance

— out of school activities (clubs, sports, etc)

— teaching provided for pupils with particular needs including special educational needs

— the use of Welsh as the language of instruction and the extent of alternative instruction in English where Welsh is used

— whether pupils must learn Welsh and whether there are any exceptions to this.

• **The school's policies on certain other matters**

In Scotland:

— enforcement of attendance

— discipline (the school rules must also be mentioned)

— homework

— wearing of uniform and certain items of other clothing (eg for gym and practical sessions). Costs of required items of uniform must be given.

In England and Wales:

— discipline and how parents are informed about school rules

— homework

— wearing of uniform and the cost of each item of uniform.

- **The school's arrangements for providing certain other services (Scotland)**

    — meals and milk, including facilities for eating packed lunches. Details must be given about entitlements to free school meals and how to claim these

    — school transport, including details of entitlement to financial help with transport costs and how to claim this

    — health care (eg visits by school doctors and specialist medical staff)

    — the school's examination results (see below).

The above topics represent the bare minimum of information about schools parents must be provided with. You may well find that information is provided on a range of other topics as well, such as the school's parent teacher or parent's association, the school fund, school equipment, library and so on.

Independent schools which belong to the assisted places scheme must also issue this information, which should also include details about their entrance requirements and fees charged.

The education authority is responsible for making sure that there is information on each school it runs and that this is brought up-to-date each year. The information is usually presented in a 'handbook', 'brochure' or 'prospectus' for each school. The school itself will often be left to decide how to present this information and how much detail to go into, although in some education authorities, schools may be required to adopt a standard cover and format in designing their handbooks.

There must be a Gaelic version for all schools in Gaelic-speaking areas and, in Wales, education authorities or the governors of voluntary schools may decide to publish the information in Welsh.
Parents of children at schools from other non-English speaking backgrounds, for example from Asian communities, may also be able to obtain copies of this information in their mother tongue, although the education authority would probably have to be satisfied that the number of parents was large enough before arranging to do this.

When the education authority tells you that it proposes to place your child in a particular school, it must supply you automatically and free of charge with a copy of information for that school. If you don't get a copy, ask for one, either by contacting the authority or the school concerned. You can also ask for a copy of the school information for any other school.

The information may be hand delivered to you via your child, if already at school. It could be posted to you directly in the case of very young children. It must be sent to you directly if your child is at a special school.

You should ask for the information about an individual school at the school itself. It has to be free of charge. Education authorities are not

30

obliged to gather this information centrally, so you may not be able to get a copy at their offices.

You can get information about a special school either at the school itself or at the offices of the education authority. Again, it will be free of charge.

You can use this information:

- to help you decide which school (if you are making a choice) would be the most suitable one for your child to attend. In England and Wales, the information must give details of arrangements for visiting the school as part of the process of choosing
- for finding out how to get in touch with the school and meet staff
- for reference when discussing your child's progress or other matters with the school staff
- to understand what the schools policies are on matters such as discipline and homework
- to help you claim any entitlements your child may have to free school meals, transport, clothing, etc.

A good school handbook should be clearly written, interesting to read, well laid out, perhaps illustrated (with drawings, diagrams etc) and generally make you as a parent feel a 'partner' with staff in your child's education. The appearance and quality of school handbooks will to some extent be affected by guidelines laid down by the education authority about how school handbooks should be produced and written and also by how much money and staff time schools can devote to them, with the result that some school handbooks are a great deal better than others.

Things to watch out for when reading handbooks include:

- obscure terminology or jargon, complicated sentences, or a formal style or tone of language which distances you from the school. Ask the school to explain educational terms you do not understand
- leaving out or glossing over important details, especially ones required by law. Does the handbook say enough about provisions for

wheelchair access, for example. Suggest to the school what other details could go in the handbook

- small type, messy print, lack of headings, poor arrangements of pages or paragraphs, pages missing. Offer your services to improve the design of the handbook!

Check that what the school says in its handbook is borne out by the school's practice, for example, reporting on children's progress to parents, and complain to the school or to the education authority if the school does not come up to its word.

In Scotland

Every secondary school must include in its information for parents the results of Scottish Certificate of Education examinations taken by pupils. The results must be set out in such a way that you can see the number of pupils in each year (fourth, fifth and sixth) achieving different grades in each subject and that these numbers are listed out of the total number of pupils in each year. They will *not* tell you how many children took each subject and therefore what the success rate was, although the school may decide to publish this information as well.

The school may publish the results of other exams taken by pupils, such as the National Certificate or English GCSE exams. The school may also put some of this information into its reports to pupils and their parents.

In England and Wales

Every secondary school must include in its information for parents its policy on entering pupils for public examinations. It must also give the previous year's examination results in such a way that you can see the number of pupils in each year achieving different grades in each subject and compare these numbers with the total number of pupils in each year.

Studying school exam results

You may be interested in studying a school's exam results:

- when deciding which secondary school your child should go to
- to find out what range of exam subjects a school has on offer and how well a school has done in particular subjects
- to work out which school subjects your own child should specialise in.

School exam results should be read with great caution, however, and if necessary be discussed with staff. Differences in exam results between schools do not necessarily mean that some schools are more efficient than others; they may be due to differences in the social backgrounds of pupils, which are known to be related to achievements. The results for one particular year may not be representative of results for previous or future years — schools have their 'ups and downs'.

⮑ For more guidance on how to study exam results of Scottish schools, see *A Parent's Guide to Examination Results* obtainable from the Scottish Council for Research in Education, 15 St John Street, Edinburgh EH8 85R.

Under proposed changes in the law announced at the time of writing, school boards (which replace school councils) will have a duty to report to parents and their communities on their activities.

Each school board must receive from the headteacher:

- a statement on the school's policies and any changes in those policies on the curriculum, the assessment of pupils, school rules and discipline, and the wearing of school uniform.

- an annual report, including a report on the level of pupils' attainments.

- any other reports which the board may from time to time reasonably require.

The education authority and the headteacher must consider any representations the board may make about this information or statements in these reports. The authority must also provide whatever information a board may reasonably request about the school or the provision of education in the authority's area.

Each school board must as often as it thinks necessary report to parents on its activities and find out what the views of parents are on matters it is responsible for.

Boards may also report on the school's efforts to promote good links between parents and staff. Parents must receive information about parental candidates seeking election as school board members.

Annual Reports

Governors have to produce an annual report on their work to be sent free of charge to every parent. The report must also give the names of all the governors, with their term of office and details of how they were appointed and whom they represent; the school's examination results; financial statements; and information about steps to improve community links. If they think it necessary, they can produce the report in other languages. The report forms the basis of the annual parents' meeting and it has to report on the outcomes of any resolutions from the previous year's meeting.

Statement of aims

Governors have to prepare a statement giving their view of the curricular aims of their school. They must also prepare a separate written statement setting out their view on whether sex education should be part of the curriculum, and on how it should be taught if it is to be taught at all. Also they have to provide parents with information about school syllabuses and other educational matters.

Official inspections are carried out on all schools — whether run by local authorities or independently — and further education and other colleges. The inspections are carried out by H.M.I.s — Her Majesty's Inspectors — who then produce a report on each school for the Secretary of State for Scotland or, for England, the Secretary of State for Education and Science or the Secretary of State for Wales.

What information do they contain?

The reports usually comment on:

- the school or college and its community
- its accommodation and resources (that is, buildings, books, equipment, and staffing)
- its management
- what is taught and teaching methods at each stage in the school and within each department
- the assessment of pupils
- what help is available for pupils with learning difficulties or other special educational needs
- guidance and social education
- home-school relations.

The reports are not usually very long.

How to get a copy

You can either ask to see a reference copy at the school or at your local library. Your PTA may also keep a reference copy. Or you can ask the school, the education authority, or the Scottish Education Department, Department of Education and Science or Welsh Office to send you a copy for your own use. Copies are free of charge. You do not have to have a child at the school to ask for a copy: you can obtain HMI reports for other schools in your area (if these are available).

⇨ HMI reports on schools are only available for up to three years after they are published. Your education authority should be able to tell you for which schools in your area reports are available.

How to use this information

An inspector's report may help you to work out a school's strengths and weaknesses, which could be important when choosing a school or discussing your child's progress with school staff. It could also form the basis for discussion at meetings of the school board or governing body or parent-teachers' association. In England and Wales the report could be discussed at the annual meeting of the school.

Drawbacks

Schools may each have their own different approaches to teaching and learning, different intakes of pupils and so on, and so it may not make sense to compare one school with another when reading inspectors' reports.

As schools or education authorities should take steps to remedy defects identified by the inspectors as soon as possible, reports may also be out of date by the time you come to read them.

You may not share the inspectors' assumptions as to what is good and desirable in a school.

Reading inspectors' reports

As inspectors' reports are not simply written for parents but for professional staff as well, they may not always use language which is easy to understand.

You may sometimes have to do quite a bit of reading between the lines to understand what is being said. You will not, for example, find a report saying "This is an awful school with an ineffectual head, narrow-minded teachers, an old-fashioned curriculum, crumbling buildings and ill-disciplined pupils". Instead you will tend to find hints that all is not well and changes need to be made in phrases such as "generally adequate" and "attention should be given to".

➥ *HM Inspectors' Reports — a guide for parents,* published by the Scottish Parent Teacher Council, offers helpful hints for reading inspectors' reports and what particular phrases might mean. For example, "attention should be given to" probably means "there is plenty of room for improvement here".

What is produced

As well as the school's handbook or brochure (see page 00), you will probably find a number of other documents produced by the school.

Secondary schools usually produce handbooks for pupils and their parents at various key stages through school — for example a booklet introducing them to the school and telling them what will happen over the first two years; another at the outset of the second two years leading up to SCE Ordinary or Standard grade or to the GCSE and A level in England and Wales, and other exams; and later a variety of booklets on further education or careers opportunities.

Primary and secondary schools often send regular newsletters or bulletins to parents, giving up-to-date information about past or forthcoming school events, activities, trips abroad, staff changes, alterations to school buildings, new equipment, etc. Some headteachers may produce an annual report (others prefer to give their report verbally at an annual event such as speech day).

Then there is the information *produced by pupils*: school magazines, newsletters, journals or special publications.

Finally there are the minutes, newsletters and any other papers produced by the school board or governing body and the parent-teacher association.

Where to obtain copies

Ask the school for all of these publications. Most are free of charge, but you may be asked to pay for a copy of the school magazine. You should also find copies of school board minutes at the education authority offices and in your local library.

Making use of school publications

School newsletters, magazines and similar publications not only give you further insight into what the school is doing but may also:

- offer handy hints or suggestions about giving your child encouragement and support at home, for example in developing new interests, completing homework, preparing for exams, etc.
- alert you to problems or difficulties the school is having, for example, in keeping the buildings in good repair, replacing old textbooks, etc.
- point to practical ways you can support the school, such as helping to run school clubs, donating books and so on.

What information can you get from the education authority?

The last two sections have been concerned with information you can obtain about your child or your child's school. This section deals with information you can get on the educational services run by your regional or islands council in Scotland — the education authority for your area — or, in England and Wales, by your local education authority. This can range from information about practical matters, such as entitlement to free school meals or financial help for young people staying on at school after 16, to information about the education authority's policies, for example on what should be taught or the education of children with special needs.

The law now gives you important rights to receive written information about education authority services.

In Scotland

You are entitled to receive three broad kinds of information:

- **basic information**   mostly practical information, such as addresses and phone numbers
- **school information**   this has already been mentioned in the previous section and so is not repeated here
- **supplementary information** mostly about the education authority's policies or practices.

In England and Wales

You are entitled to receive two kinds of information:

- **general information**   details of the local services and information about policies and procedures
- **school information**   see the previous section.

In addition, education authorities have to set out their policies on the secular curriculum in their schools. They must give a copy to headteachers and governors, but they can publish it more widely.

You are also normally entitled to see the papers, agendas and minutes of council, committee and subcommittee meetings, including, in most cases, background reports prepared by council officials.

What does basic information cover?

- information about schools in the education authority's area (for example, a school's name, address, telephone number, size)

- how the authority decides which school a child will go to

- the authority's policies and arrangements for offering school places

- contact names and numbers of officials in the education department who can advise parents about such matters as asking for a choice of school or making an appeal

- contact name(s)/number(s) of officials who can help parents of children needing special help with their education, such as children with physical or mental disabilities or other problems

- where to get supplementary information from (see below)

- policy on school meals, school transport, boarding facilities etc.

The information must be updated each year.

Basic information must be given to you in writing; this could come in a single publication, such as a booklet, or could be in separate sections, such as information sheets. Make it clear what items of information you are interested in.

There must be a Gaelic version of the information in all Gaelic-speaking areas, that is, the Western Isles, parts of Skye and Lochalsh and some other Highlands and Islands areas.

How to obtain this information

Basic information should be available for you to see free of charge at:

- your local education offices
- public libraries
- at any education authority school.

You can ask for your own copy of basic information if:

- you have a child living in the education authority's area

- your child is about to move to the area
- you have told the authority that you intend to send your child to school in the area.

You can ask for basic information relating to any number of schools in the area to which your child might go.

How can basic information be used

Basic information can be useful to you, for example, if you want to:

- send your child to a school outside the area you live in
- know what the authority's policy is on providing school meals, hostels, transport and so on
- know what the authority's policy is for allowing your child to start school at an earlier age, before $4^1/_2$ to 5
- know who is who within the education department.

You can find out about education and schools in your area through the *basic* and *school* information. But there is also a lot of other information, called *supplementary information* about a whole range of other matters which you may ask to be given to you. Most of this is about schooling throughout the authority's area and not just particular schools.

What does this sort of information cover?

Information about:

- the area from which schools normally take pupils (maps showing these areas can be seen at your local education offices and schools)
- which primary schools normally send pupils to which secondary schools
- how the authority deals with placing requests and appeals — that is, requests or appeals from parents for a child to go to a particular school
- how the authority fixes the maximum number of pupils for any school or a particular school or class, primary or secondary
- general policy and practice on curriculum and examinations
- arrangements for educating children who have special aptitudes, for example, in music
- arrangements for educating children with special educational needs
- independent special schools used by the education authority
- nursery education
- schools in which Gaelic is taught.

and also general policy on:

- enforcement of school attendance
- school milk and meals, and charging for them
- school uniform
- school transport
- financial help towards clothing, shoes, equipment etc.
- bursaries and maintenance allowances
- discipline and school rules

- school boards (structure, membership, functions and who is on the school council relating to any particular school).

This information may be provided verbally, but must then be given to you in written form if you so request. You should make it clear which item of supplementary information you want.

Some authorities publish their supplementary information in booklet form, while in others it will appear in several documents.

The authority is expected to keep supplementary information up-to-date as much as possible.

If asked the authority can (but does not have to) supply supplementary information in a language other than English.

Who can receive supplementary information?

If you are the parent of a child living, or proposing to live, in the education authority's area, or you have told the authority that you are considering making a placing request, you are entitled to be given any item of supplementary information which you ask for free of charge. In some cases you may be asked to put your request in writing.

The education authority can send the information home via your child; this information need not be mailed to you directly, except if your child goes to a special school.

Information about choice of school

There are special rules about what information must be provided if you ask for your own choice of school, that is you make a 'placing request'. You must normally be told of:

- your right to ask for a place at a school or schools other than the one(s) offered to your child. Normally this will happen before your child is due to start or transfer school
- the person or body dealing with your request and whether or not you will be given a chance to present your case verbally or in writing
- the grounds on which the authority may turn down your request
- your rights of appeal to an appeal committee, if your request is turned down, and your further rights of appeal to the sheriff court.

You must be sent this information within five working days of your placing request being received.

Details of when, how and where to make placing requests must be advertised in local newspapers at least once a year — usually at least six months before the next school starting or transfer date and not later than four weeks before the final date for making placing requests.

General information covers:

- **Admission arrangements**
  - the number of pupils to be admitted to the school
  - the role of the education authority and of the governors in admission procedures
  - the education authority's policy on admissions
  - arrangements for admitting pupils who live outside the education authority's area
  - the criteria for offering places at non-maintained schools
  - the arrangements for allowing parents to express the preference for the school of their choice and to appeal against a school admission decision
  - the arrangements for transferring between schools other than at normal admission age.

- **Factual information about the authority and its schools**
  - the addresses and phone numbers of the authority's offices
  - how parents can get hold of information about individual schools
  - the names, addresses and telephone numbers of every school
  - the number of pupils at each school and their age range
  - the classification of each school (primary, middle, secondary or sixth form college; comprehensive, secondary modern, grammar or bilateral; coeducational or single-sex; day or boarding or both)
  - the denominational status of each school.

- **Information about welfare benefits**
  - policies and arrangements on school transport including details of the provision of free transport and help with transport costs
  - policies and arrangements on providing school clothing (including uniform and gym and sports clothing) and clothing grants and an address where parents can get help
  - grants for other expenses (for example, the cost of field trips) and allowances for pupils over the age of 16, and the address where parents can get further information.

- **General policy on entering pupils for examinations**

- **In Wales, general policy on Welsh language use**
  - the authority's policy on the use of the Welsh language in its schools and by pupils of all or different age groups, particularly on the use of Welsh as the language of instruction, whether pupils have to learn Welsh and if there are any exemptions.

- **Special education**
  - how children with special educational needs are assessed and parents involved in the assessment process
  - provision for children with special educational needs in ordinary and special schools and in schools in other authorities
  - special educational provision provided other than at school
  - policies and arrangements for using non-maintained and independent schools for children with special needs
  - how parents can get advice if they think their child may have

special educational needs

— arrangements for transport to and from special schools and independent schools

— how parents can get information about individual special schools.

For most parents the basic, school and supplementary information (Scotland) or the general and school information (England and Wales) should answer most questions about your child's schooling or education in your area. However, a lot of educational matters are also covered by council papers, committee reports and other documents, which the education authority will refer to in reaching decisions or putting them into practice, as shown in the diagram below.

The council decision-making route

education officials
produce background papers or reports

education committee or subcommittee
considers reports and papers,
and any subcommittee recommendations
and makes a decision

council
approves (or rejects) the
education committee's decision

officials
carry out council's decisions

It is possible to follow how these decisions are reached much more closely than before. You can now:

- attend meetings of the council, its committees and subcommittees
- ⇨ You can be excluded, however, if the meeting is discussing information supplied in confidence by a government department or

information whose disclosure is prohibited by law or a court order. This can also happen while certain matters, such as salaries, are being discussed. The exclusion applies only to that particular item of business and not to the whole meeting — unless the whole meeting is on these confidential matters.

- see and receive your own copies of various documents *before* the meeting

  You must be shown the notice giving the time and place of the meeting, the agenda, and you can ask for copies of any reports likely to be considered in public and background papers used in preparing these reports. These documents should be available at least three days before a meeting and in some authorities they may be available even earlier.

- see documents *at* the meeting

  A reasonable number of copies of the agenda and any reports to be considered in public must be available for handing out to the public attending

- see documents *after* the meeting

  You can inspect the agenda, any reports considered in public, background papers, and minutes of the meeting (or a summary of those parts considered when the meeting was closed to the public).

You can see background papers going back up to four years, and other documents going back up to six years before the date of the meeting. You can also inspect a list of the names and addresses of councillors, and of the membership of the education committee and any subcommittees, and a list of powers delegated to officers.

How to obtain these documents

You can see or obtain your own copies of any of these documents at the main offices of your education authority. You may be charged for looking at background papers, but all other documents must be open to inspection without charge. You are entitled to a photocopy of any document open to inspection, but will probably have to pay for these.

Copies of education committee and subcommittee minutes — but probably not background papers — should also be in your local or central library.

When reading committee (or subcommittee) minutes, you should note whether a firm *decision* has been made on the agenda item you are interested in, or whether a line of action has merely been *recommended*. You will have to check the minutes of the full council (or committee) to find out which recommendations have been *approved*. You may also have to go back to previous minutes or reports to understand what has gone on before.

Subjects which are discussed by the education committee/subcommittee

Typical items on an education committee agenda are likely to include:

- educational expenditure
- school closures
- school buildings
- school meals and transport
- new examinations.

There may also be one-off debates, for example on how to improve the education of children from different racial or cultural backgrounds, or what information to give pupils on AIDS, drug abuse etc.

Education authorities are staffed by officials, led by a director of education or chief education officer, whose work is mainly with councillors, school staff, civil servants and other officials. But they also deal with enquiries from parents and you should not hesitate to approach them if you cannot get the information or advice you want from the school.

The first hurdle to cross is knowing which official to deal with. If your enquiry is about a choice of school or your child's special educational needs, you may already have been given the name of an official to contact for advice and information.

Otherwise, writing to the director of education, chief education officer or divisional education officer should ensure your enquiry reaches the right official, though you may not get a reply straight away. Phoning up or calling in person may result in your enquiry being attended to promptly but it may take some time to track down the right official. You could ask for a list of who's who in the department for future reference.

Think carefully about what you want to say before writing or phoning. Are you, for example, wanting information about a particular school or are you more interested in information about a policy affecting more than one school, such as information about starting or transferring school?

If you are given information over the phone, you can ask for the official to send you a written copy as well, but in certain circumstances you may be asked to pay for this. If you want a written reply to your questions, it is sometimes better to start by writing rather than phoning, then the authority's reply has to be in writing. Keep copies of your own letters.

If you have difficulty in getting the information you want and this information you seek is of general interest to other parents in your area, it might be worth getting help from:

- your parents' representative on the school board or governing body

- your parents' group (PTA or PA)

- your regional or islands councillor (Scotland) or local education authority member (England and Wales).

These people or bodies may agree to approach the officials themselves for the information you want.

Many of the arrangements for educating children in your area are based on the policies of the education authority, which has a lot of discretion to decide how schooling should be provided.

The authority is nevertheless influenced by the policies of central government, for example in deciding what is to be taught and what exams pupils should sit. In certain cases, the authority is also bound by certain legal requirements, for example consulting parents before it can close down a school.

You or your parents' group can find out what central government policy or the law on education is by looking at:

- reports, policy documents (such as 'green' and 'white' papers) issued by the Scottish Office and related bodies, such as the Scottish Education Department, Consultative Committee on the Curriculum, by the Department of Education and Science (DES) and by the Welsh Office, and so on
- government legislation — in acts of parliament and regulations — which enforces government policies
- government circulars advising education authorities how to put legislation into practice or drawing attention to other developments
- reports in the press or education journals summarising or commenting on government policies.

There is a regular flow of reports, consultation papers and policy documents coming from the Scottish Office, DES and Welsh Office. These can provide useful factual details as well as information on the government's thinking or approach to a particular matter.

Before a government introduces legislation or makes other changes to carry out its policies, it may spend some time seeking views from a wide range of people. It may produce various 'consultative' documents to sound out the views of various bodies about a problem or issue. In other cases, though, it may decide to legislate straight away, and then it becomes important to make your views known to Members of Parliament.

Types of policy document

- Green papers
  These set out policy proposals and invite discussion before any new laws or other changes are made

- White papers
  These take into account the responses to any green paper which preceded them and, if changes in the law are planned, set out or summarise the proposed legislation. For example, there was a white paper on the education of children with special needs.

- Parliamentary debates
  Hansard, obtainable through government bookshops and libraries, gives verbatim reports of all parliamentary debates. It comes with a separate index to help you find debates about topics you are interested in, for example, on an education bill.

- Other policy and consultative papers
  The Scottish Education Department also publishes a wide range of reports and policy papers, for example on research findings, or proposals for changes in examinations or courses. Recent examples in Scotland have included consultative documents on the role of parents in school management and on curriculum and assessment policies.

  The DES and Welsh Office have recently consulted on, for example, proposals for a national curriculum, greater control over school finances by governors, and giving schools the right to 'opt out' of local authority control.

How to obtain government documents

Most major government documents, such as green and white papers, are obtainable through government bookshops, but major libraries should stock copies as well. A classified list of these is found in *Government Publications Sectional Lists for England, Scotland* and *Wales.* Ask a librarian for help if you are having difficulty tracing a government publication.

Not all government publications are available through government bookshops or appear in the above mentioned list. However, government departments issue many reports and policy papers of their own which are not put on general sale to the public. You can nevertheless order or ask to see many of these publications by writing to or phoning the publications service of the Scottish Office Library at New St Andrew's House, Edinburgh EH1 3TD, which also issues its own list of Scottish Office publications or, in England and Wales, The Publications Despatch Centre, Government Buildings, Honeypot Lane, Stanmore, Middlesex HA7 1AZ.

Most major official publications are summarised or reported on in the national press, including the education pages of *The Glasgow Herald, The Guardian, The Independent,* and *The Scotsman. The Times Educational*

Supplement and *The Times Educational Supplement Scotland* also give detailed coverage of most educational reports. *ACE Bulletin*, published by the Advisory Centre for Education, contains a digest of recent government publications of educational interest to parents. A new journal *School Governor* also covers topics of relevance to parents and others involved in the running of schools.

How to use government policy documents

You or your parents' group should feel free to make your views known about proposed policy changes and not be put off by the fact that 'consultations' often take place between government and various 'official' bodies. The views of any group with a legitimate interest will usually be welcomed.

You can:

- write your own submission to the government giving your views
- ask to meet government or other official representatives to put your views across, including meetings with ministers or influential backbenchers on matters of very serious concern
- prepare articles or make statements to the press, radio and TV
- run a more prolonged campaign (meetings with the government, press statements, public meetings and perhaps demonstrations)
- see your own MP
- liaise with other parents' groups, possibly through the Scottish Parent Teacher Council, or in England and Wales, the National Confederation of Parent Teacher Associations and the Campaign for the Advancement of State Education.

Act of Parliament

The laws that govern us are the Acts of parliament. An act or 'statute' starts as a draft, called a 'bill' which is debated in the House of Commons and House of Lords before it is approved by the Queen (given 'Royal Assent') and becomes an act.

You will find the following acts of parliament to be of particular relevance when seeking information on educational matters.

In Scotland

Education (Scotland) Act 1980

> The main act setting out the legal rights and responsibilities of both parents and education authorities on a wide range of educational matters.

Education (Scotland) Act 1981

> This amends the 1980 Act and in particular makes clear your right to ask for your own choice of school, to be consulted before a school can be closed down, to receive written information and other matters of direct interest to parents.

⇨ As Scotland has its own system of law, it is important to consult acts or parts of acts applying to Scotland. Acts applying to Scotland have "(Scotland)" written into their titles. Some acts covering the whole of Britain may nonetheless include parts that apply specifically to Scotland, for example, laws dealing with race and sex discrimination in Scottish education. Some acts for "England and Wales" also contain sections which extend or apply only to Scotland, for example, the sections in the 1986 Education Act outlawing corporal punishment.

In England and Wales

Education Act 1944

> The main act providing the framework for the education system in England and Wales.

Education Act 1980

This lays down procedures on school admissions (including the obligation on schools and education authorities to provide information for parents and the right of parents to 'express a preference' for the school of their choice and to appeal against decisions on admissions); attendance; the establishment, alteration and closure of schools; and on school government.

Education Act 1981

This covers the education of children with special educational needs and gives parents greater rights of involvement in the assessment process.

Education (No. 2) Act 1986

This defines new responsibilities for governing bodies, extending their role and setting out their composition.

In Scotland, England and Wales

Local Government (Access to Information) Act 1985

This gives members of the public a right of access to the meetings and papers of local councils and their committees and subcommittees, and therefore increases your right to see documents on education policy and practice.

⇨ At the time of writing two further education bills, one for Scotland, the other for England and Wales, were being considered by parliament. The Scottish bill provides for the setting up of school boards, the bill for England and Wales covers the national curriculum, school 'opting out' from local authority control and other matters.

Government regulations

Often an act of parliament states the broad principle of the law, but leaves the details to be set out in regulations, known as *Statutory Instruments*. These regulations carry just as much force as an act of parliament, but do not have to go through the same lengthy process: they come into force simply by being published and 'laid before' (announced in) parliament. Statutory Instruments are also used to bring acts of parliament into force.

For example, changes in the law providing information for parents were brought about by *The Education (Scotland) Act 1981*, but the details are found in *The Education (School and Placing Information) (Scotland) Regulations 1982*. For England and Wales, the act was *The Education Act 1980* and the Statutory Instruments *The Education (School Information) Regulations 1981*.

Parliamentary legislation is difficult to read and the gist of what it sets out is often better understood by reading other books which explain it. This is what the SCC's *The Law of the School* sets out to do for Scotland. The Advisory Centre for Education (ACE) publishes readable guides to education law in England and Wales. In Scotland there are also government leaflets, for example on your rights on choice of school. So as an individual parent you will probably not need to read much legislation. You may however want to refer to the legislation itself if you become involved in lengthy and complicated issues such as appealing against a decision not to admit your child to the school of your choice, or — together with other parents — fighting a decision to close your local school.

If you are going to make use of any of the education acts, it is almost essential to read the regulations too: for they really are part of the same legislation. Regulations tend (though not always) to be written in somewhat less complicated English.

You will be able to get help in understanding your legal position from your local advice centres (though centres are unlikely to keep copies of the legislation itself) or a local solicitor (who should have copies of the acts, though possibly not the regulations that go with them).

And it might be useful too if some members of your parents' group could gain sufficient expertise in finding their way round and understanding these documents to help others. Some guidance about reading legislation is given in the following pages.

You should be able to look at reference copies of most of the important acts in your local library or at the main office of the education authority. You may find a solicitor who will allow you to look at his or her copy without charging you. Your child's school, the PTA, school council or governing body may also already carry a reference copy. You can buy your own copy, usually between £5 and £10, from the government bookshops (see cover). Regulations may be harder to get hold of, but the main offices of your education authority may let you consult their own copies. You can buy copies of regulations in the same way as acts of parliament, from government bookshops.

Reading acts of parliament

All acts start with a list of their contents, which sets out the following:

title	A title such as *The Education (Scotland) Act 1981* indicates that the Act applies only to Scotland and became law in 1981.
chapter	All statutes are 'chapters' within the complete 'statute book' of all acts of parliament.
sections	Acts of parliament are all divided into sections which may consist of one or several subsections. If there are a lot of sections or the act covers different topics, these sections may be arranged in different Parts (like chapters of a book).
	You will see when you go to a particular section that it can be further subdivided into subsections (1), (2), (3) … and so on. These can be further subdivided into (a), (b), (c) … and so on. And there are even further subdivisions into (i), (ii), (iii) …!
schedules	These are found at the end of an act, and are like appendices in a book: they are used to spell out subjects in greater detail, or to give lists, and to give details such as how other legislation is affected by this act.

example of top of front page

STATUTORY INSTRUMENTS

1982 NO 950 (S. 125)

EDUCATION, SCOTLAND

The Education (School and Placing Information) (Scotland) Regulations 1982

Made - - - -	9th July 1982
Laid before Parliament	20th July 1982
Coming into Operation	1st January 1983

You can refer to these regulations as SI 1982/950 *The Education (School and Placing Information) (Scotland) Regulations 1982.*

SI is short for statutory instrument;

950 is the reference number of this particular SI;

(S.125 is the reference number of the series of purely Scottish regulations).

The statutory instrument is then broken up into a series of regulations (these are referred to by their regulation number, not section number as with an act of parliament). There may also be schedules at the end, as with an act. Unlike acts of parliament, regulations end with a short explanatory note, which will often help you to understand what they are about.

The language of statutes and regulations

In order not to be open to misinterpretation and to cover for all possible situations, legislation tends to be written in what appears to the lay reader as very formal and convoluted language.

Although you may at first be put off by this from reading legislation, with a little practice it *is* nonetheless possible to get used to the style of legislation and to come to grips with what it means. There is a side benefit to this: the more you grapple with laws, the more you can understand the way the minds of politicians, officials and lawyers work and can respond to — or challenge — their statements with more confidence.

examples

"shall"	this really means "must" — there is no choice — this is an order by parliament.
"may"	someone is allowed to do it but does not have to.
"hereinafter"	in what follows.
"subject to subsection (2) below"	what follows will be the case except in situations covered by subsection (2). So you have to read this subsection and subsection (2) to get the full picture.

This is true in general about reading legislation. Apart from needing a dictionary at your side, you will need all your fingers to keep open various pages of the act, for it will constantly refer you to other sections or to schedules in the act.

Other things to look for:

• **amendments to other legislation**

 Somewhere near the end of the Act, there will be a section describing how this Act amends or repeals (replaces) previous acts. Thus *The Education (Scotland) Act 1982* amends the 1980 Act, which is therefore often referred to as "*The Education (Scotland) Act 1980 as amended.* ."

• **extent**

 Again, usually towards the end of the Act there will be a section which says which parts of the United Kingdom the law covers (that is "the extent" of the Act). Sometimes only certain sections apply to Scotland, not the whole Act. If an act does not say which parts of the United Kingdom it extends to, then it applies to all parts of the UK.

• **date of commencement**

 Just because a law has received Royal Assent does not mean that it will immediately come into force: there may have to be a delay while government and local government departments make the necessary arrangements for the changes. For this reason the act may state — again in a section at the end of the act — a date of implementation a few months on from the date of Royal Assent. Or it may say the act will "come into force on such a day as the Secretary of State may by order made by statutory instrument appoint". This is known as "the appointed day".

- **repeal of legislation**

    "Repeal" and "Revoke" mean the same thing: to end. Acts are repealed; orders or statutory instruments are revoked.

Pitfalls when reading legislation

Part of the act or regulation you are reading may not yet have come into force. Or it may have been changed by later acts or regulations.

You may need to refer to court cases to understand how the law has been interpreted; not all cases are reported however.

The laws may misrepresent actual practices. Some education authorities may do *more* than the law strictly requires, provided they do not act beyond what they are allowed to do. Other authorities may apply the law grudgingly or in half-hearted fashion.

A lot of what education authorities or schools do, for example in deciding how children should be taught, is not governed by law at all.

Court decisions on educational matters

Laws passed by parliament affect how the education system is run. Occasionally there are disputes about how the laws should be interpreted. In these cases it is the courts that decide what the law means.

Sometimes these disputes happen because the law may be genuinely unclear, on other occasions they may arise because people are not happy with the law as it stands and want it changed. Thus during the late seventies there were several cases in Scotland in which parents went to the sheriff court to force the education authority to let them send their child to the school of their choice. This period ended with the government deciding to provide a clearer statement about parental choice in the *Education (Scotland) Act 1981*.

Further information

Central libraries should stock copies of legislation and the reference books below, or you could ask the librarian where you could get copies from. Bear in mind, though, that not all court cases are published ('reported') and that one court case is not necessarily legally binding on another.

In Scotland

For information about laws currently in force, recent changes in the law and past court cases, you or your solicitor will need to refer to such publications as the *Scottish Current Law Year Book, Current Law Statutes: Scottish edition* and the *Scots Law Times*, all published by W. Green and Son. Entries are arranged by topic, for example, "Education law".

In England

For further information about laws currently in force in England and Wales, consult *The Law of Education* or *Halsbury's Statutes*, both published by Butterworths.

The Scottish Education Department (SED), the Department of Education and Science (DES) and the Welsh Office send a steady flow of circulars to education authorities. They are used not only to back up legislation but also to give local authorities further information and advice on how to implement government policy.

These circulars are usually much easier to follow than the laws or regulations which they describe, and they often explain the principles or objectives behind a new law or procedure.

It can be extremely useful therefore to get a copy of a government circular if you are trying to understand the official position on an issue such as school admissions or curriculum reform.

You can either apply to one of the following addresses for a free copy of a circular or your education authority may also agree to let you see (though not take away) their own copy.

In Scotland

To find out what circulars have been issued on various educational matters in Scotland, refer to *The Law of the School* or to the *List of Departmental Circulars and Memoranda*, obtainable free from:

> The Scottish Education Department,
> Room 323,
> 43 Jeffrey Street,
> Edinburgh EH1 1DN.

You can also write to the above address for copies of the circulars you want. (Although these circulars are intended mainly for education authorities and other official bodies, they can be given to ordinary members of the public as well.)

In England:

> DES Publications Despatch Centre,
> Government Buildings,
> Honeypot Lane, Stanmore,
> Middlesex HA7 1AZ

In Wales:

> Welsh Office,
> Education Department,
> Crown Buildings,
> Cathays Park,
> Cardiff CF1 3NQ

As well as government research and discussion documents, there are reports on educational issues coming out of university departments, the Consultative Committee on the Curriculum, the School Curriculum Development Committee for England and Wales/National Curriculum Council/Curriculum Council for Wales, the Scottish Council for Research in Education, the National Foundation for Educational Research, organisations such as the Scottish Consumer Council, the National Consumer Council and the Welsh Consumer Council, the Scottish Community Education Council and the Scottish Parent Teacher Council. Statistical information about education is regularly published by the Scottish Education Department and the DES in their *Statistical Bulletins*. The addresses of these and other bodies are given at the end.

Again, the national and educational press are likely to contain coverage of these.

Part Two: Using the information

5 Dealing with your child's schooling

This section picks out some of the problems you may face as an individual parent with a child at school. In each case there is a list of the various types of information that you might find helpful. Obviously the list is not exhaustive, but it is intended to show you that with a little persistence and investigation, you may be able to get more information than you had first suspected was available.

When choosing a school it would be useful to have:

basic information (Scotland)

> to find out the names, addresses and phone numbers of appropriate schools in your area

supplementary information (Scotland)

> to find out where these schools are, the areas from which they normally take pupils and the education authority's policy and procedures for dealing with placing requests

general information (England and Wales)

> to find out the names, addresses and phone numbers of schools, the numbers of pupils to be admitted and the education authority's procedures for allowing you to 'express a preference' for the school of your choice

school information

> to help you make your choice of the school or schools you think might be suitable (you might also want information on another school in a different area for comparison)

school board/governing body information

> for details of the school's aims, policies, achievements, arrangements for improving home-school-community links, and so on

school magazine/newsletters

> to get a more informal insight into the school's character, say when you have narrowed the choice down to two schools

recent HMI reports

> to find out how the experts judge the school's strengths and weaknesses

government leaflets (Scotland)

> for example, in Scotland, *Choosing a School* and *The Assisted Places Scheme*, and in England and Wales, *Assisted Places in Independent Schools*

other publications

> booklets for parents on what to look for when choosing a school, such as Felicity Taylor's *Choosing a School*, published by the Advisory Centre for Education

legislation

> see Section on "Choice of School" in *The Law of the School or ACE's School Choice Appeals Handbook.*

As well as collecting this information, make an appointment to *visit the school* to talk to the headteacher and to see for yourself what facilities the school has and what impressions you get of the atmosphere when you are being taken round. Schools may arrange special 'open days' or parents' evenings at certain times of the year to enable parents to do so.

Look at:

school information

about arrangements for parents to visit and be introduced to the school; information about what is taught at the start of schooling; links between primary and secondary schools

basic information (Scotland)

about school starting dates and admission procedures; information about priorities for the early admission of children who have not reached school age

supplementary information (Scotland)

about which secondary school pupils will normally transfer to

general information (England and Wales)

about admission procedures; about transferring between schools at other than the normal admission times

other publications

about children's early years of schooling (ask your librarian about books written for parents of children starting school).

It would be helpful to have:

school report

   to find out how well your child is doing in schoolwork so far

school record

   to discover whether your child has any difficulties or problems affecting his or her schoolwork you should know about

school information

   to find out what the school's arrangements and practices are for reporting on the progress of pupils to parents and what are its arrangements for you to visit the school to discuss your child's progress

supplementary information (Scotland)

   to find out what the education authority's policies are on assessing and reporting on pupils' progress

other publications

   any recent inspector's reports on the school

legislation

   section on the "Examinations and Assessment" in *The Law of the School.*

Look at the:

school report

> to find out how well your child has done in particular subjects or areas of study so far

school record

> to discover whether your child has any difficulties or problems which could affect progress in particular subjects

school information

> to find out what choices are available and what arrangements are made for allowing pupils to make their own choices and consulting parents about these

supplementary information (Scotland)

> to find out about the education authority's policies on subject choices and selecting pupils for examinations

general information (England and Wales)

> to find out about the education authority's policies on entering pupils for examinations

other publications

> school booklets on subject choice and related career choices; college or university prospectuses giving details of entry requirements

legislation

> sections on "Curriculum" and "Examinations and Assessment" in *The Law of the School* and on "Curriculum" in the *ACE Summary of the Education (No 2) Act 1986.*

Look at the:

school reports or progress records

> to see how your child performed in particular tests or exams

school handbook

> to find out how groups of pupils performed in SCE, GCSE and other public examinations

supplementary or general information

> for details of the education authority's policies and practices about entering pupils for examinations

other publications

> Scottish Information Office publications, such as *Setting New Standards for All Pupils* (about the SCE Standard Grade Examination) and, for England and Wales, *GCSE: a General Introduction*, HMSO, 1985.

Look at the:

school report

> to find out what your child's learning difficulties are, for example, in reading and spelling

school record

> to understand better how the school has reached its conclusions, particularly if your opinion of your child's capabilities differs dramatically from the school's

Record of Needs (Scotland) or
Statement of Special Educational Needs (England and Wales)

> to see exactly what the school and education authority think the problems are, and what help they propose to offer

school information

> to find out what special help (if any) is on offer at the school

supplementary information (Scotland) or
general information (England and Wales)

> to find out what the education authority's general policy is on helping children with special educational needs

other publications

> the Scottish Education Department's booklet *Special Educational Needs: a Guide for Parents*, the Advisory Centre for Education's *Special Education Handbook*, and various leaflets or booklets produced by professional and voluntary organisations concerned with your child's difficulties

legislation

> section on "Special Educational Needs" in *The Law of the School* (Scotland) and the *Special Education Handbook* (England and Wales).

Look at:

school reports

> to find out whether your child has made exceptional progress in certain activities, such as music, art, mathematics, science, technical subjects, etc

school information

> to find out what extra opportunities are available for children with special aptitudes or gifts, for example, specialist tuition

supplementary information (Scotland)

> to find out what the education authority's policies are for providing educational opportunities for children with special gifts or aptitudes, such as the provision of special courses

other publications

> booklets and leaflets produced by bodies such as the Gifted Children's Information Centre and library books on educating gifted children

legislation

> section on "Special Abilities and Aptitudes" in *The Law of the School.*

Look at the:

school report

> to see how much progress your child is making in spoken or written language

school information

> to find out what special help the school can provide, such as extra language tuition

supplementary information (Scotland) and
general information (England and Wales)

> to find out what the education authority's policy is on how to help your child and if there is any teaching in your child's first language
>
> ⇨ You can ask for this information to be provided in your own language, although the authority will probably only agree to this if similar requests are made by a sufficient number of other parents

legislation

> section on "Bilingual Education" in Scotland in *The Law of the School.*

Look at:

basic information

> to find out which schools in your area use Gaelic
>
> ➷ You can ask for this information to be written in Gaelic

school information

> to find out what use is made of Gaelic at the school and how much instruction is in English. The school information should be written in Gaelic and English

school report

> to find out how much progress your child is making in spoken and written Gaelic and English

supplementary information

to find out what the education authority's policies or practices are for educating children from any Gaelic speaking communities in its area

other publications

free "*Summary of the Report of an Independent Evaluation of the Western Isles Bilingual Education Project*", obtainable from the Scottish Office Library, Publications Section.

Dè mu dheidhinn na Gàidhlig?

Is dòcha gu bheil sibh a' fuireach sa Ghaidhealtachd, no am measg Ghaidheil. Is dòcha gu bheil sibh airson gum biodh a' Ghàidhlig aig ur clann, ged nach eil i agaibhsi.

Sa chiad àite:

Faighnichibh dè na sgoiltean san sgìre agaibh anns am bi teagasg Gàidhlig.

San sgoil:

Faighnichibh am bi iad a' teagasg na Gàidhlig mar chuspair, no am bi iad a' teagasg anns a' Ghàidhlig — se sin, a' teagasg chuspairean troimh mheadhan na Gàidhlig.

San iomradh-sgoile:

Gheibh sibh fios an seo ciamar a tha ur clann a' faighinn air adhart ann a bhith a' sgrìobhadh is a' bruidhinn na Gàidhlig.

Agus mu dheireadh:

Faighnichibh dè am poileasaidh a th'aig Roinn an Fhoghlaim san sgìre agaibh a thaobh oideachas na Gàidhlig.

Foillseachaidhean eile:

Gheibh sibh geàrr-chunntas air iomradh na h-ionnsaigh dà-chànanaich sna h-Eileanan an Iar an-asgaidh bho Leabharlann Oifis na h-Albann, Roinn an Fhoillseachaidh.

Look at:

general information

> to find out about your authority's policy on the use of Welsh as the language of instruction in the schools in your area, whether pupils have to learn Welsh and whether there are any exceptions to this rule.

> If the authority thinks it necessary, this information can be published in Welsh.

school information

> to find out about the use of Welsh as the language of instruction, whether pupils have to learn Welsh and whether there are exceptions to this rule. There may also be a Welsh version of the school information.

school report

> to find out how much progress your child is making in spoken and written Welsh and English.

Darllenwch:

- *y wybodaeth cyffredinol*

  i ddarganfod polisi eich awdurdod ynglyn â dysgu drwy gyfrwng y Gymraeg, dysgu Cymraeg fel pwnc i bob disgybl ac os oes eithriadau i'r rheol hon.

  Mae modd cyhoeddi'r wybodaeth yn Gymraeg os yn nhyb yr awdurdod y dylid gwneud hyn.

- *y wybodaeth am yr ysgol*

  i weld os defnyddir y Gymraeg fel cyfrwng dysgu, os oes rhaid i ddisgyblion ddysgu Cymraeg ac os oes eithriadau i'r rheol hon. Mae'n bosib y bydd y wybodaeth ar gael yn Gymraeg.

- *yr adroddiad ysgol*

  i weld sut mae eich plentyn yn dod ymlaen wrth ddysgu siarad ac ysgrifennu Cymraeg a Saesneg.

Check the:

school report

> to pick up any signs that your child is misbehaving or has some other problem at school

school information

> for the school policy on discipline and members of school staff (eg guidance teacher) with whom you can discuss your child's problems

other publications

> Scottish Education Department report on *Truancy and Indiscipline* (Pack Report), HMSO, 1977

legislation

> section on "Discipline and Punishment" in *The Law of the School*.

Check the:

school report
> to find out how many days your child has been absent from school, say over the past year; school staff will also be able to give you this information

school record
> to find out about any difficulties your child might be having which may be connected with his or her absence from school, especially if truancy has occurred

supplementary information (Scotland)
> to find out about the education authority's arrangements for enforcing school attendance

legislation
section on "Attendance" in *The Law of the School.*

Look at:

school information

> to see what arrangements the school makes for giving careers guidance; handbooks issued by the school about subject or careers choice

other publications

> issued through the careers advice service of the education authority for information about particular careers; guides for parents written by the Careers Research and Advisory Centre, Bateman Street, Cambridge CB2 1LZ.

legislation

> section on "Guidance" in *The Law of the School.*

6 Dealing with wider educational issues in your community

The well being of your child at school and issues of wider community concern are closely linked. For example, how well schools in your area are equipped, funded or staffed could make a lot of difference to your child's education. This chapter offers a few suggestions for putting written information to good use when you or groups of parents are concerned with some aspect of educational services in your area.

Look at:

school or PTA/PA newsletters

>   to find out what problems your school is having, for example
>   shortages of staff, books or equipment, and disrepairs

education committee, school board or governors' minutes

>   to find out what attention has been given to these difficulties or
>   problems

school information

>   for information on what is currently available in the school, for
>   example, how many specialist teachers there are

recent HMI reports

>   to identify where the experts also think that there is room for
>   improvement

local government papers

>   to find out what the education committee policy is on financing
>   schools, and information on particular issues, such as money available
>   for structural repairs

other publications

>   to find out what views people have about desirable standards in our
>   schools, such as articles or letters in the local press. See also the
>   sections on "Books, Materials and Equipment", "Class Size and
>   Staffing", "School Buildings" and other topics in *The Law of the School*,
>   and the ACE Information Sheet, *Is your LEA fulfilling its duties?*

Look at:

- *education authority and school board/governors' minutes and reports*

  to find out how much money the education authority proposes to spend or has spent on various services (staffing, buildings, books, equipment etc)

- *school, parents' or community newsletters etc.*

  to find out at first hand where more money needs to be spent

- *reports in the local or national press* (including *The Times Educational Supplement* and *The Times Educational Supplement Scotland*)

  to find out what various groups of people are saying about education spending

- *manifestos, election leaflets and other publications produced by the various political parties about spending in education*

- *government or other published figures showing how much has been spent on education*

  for example, figures in the annual *Rating Review* published by the Chartered Institute of Public Finance and Accountancy (CIPFA), Scottish Branch and CIPFA's *Estimates and Actuals* for England and Wales

- *other publications*

  section on "Finance and Funding" in *The Law of the School.*

Look at:

- *minutes and papers of your regional or islands council (Scotland) or local education authority (England and Wales)*

  to find out what is proposed (and attend meetings to hear what councillors say and to lobby them)

- *the local press*

  for reports on council and education committee meetings and what decisions (if any) were taken

- *any reports or statistics*

  considered by the council, education committee or special subcommittees in reaching any decisions about whether to close a school

- *other publications*

  the section on "School Closures and Other Changes" in *The Law of the School* and the SCC/Rural Forum publication *Making the Case for Rural Schools*, 1986.

Look at:

- *minutes of school board or governors' meetings*

  for a better understanding of how the school is run

- *reports, handbooks, newsletters produced by your child's school*

  combined with visits to the school if possible to find out about how your child is being educated

- *booklets, magazines and newsletters issued by bodies such as the Scottish Parent Teacher Council and the Advisory Centre for Education*

  for advice and information about parental involvement, including setting up parents' groups

- *books and national reports dealing with home-school relations*

  your library may stock some of these or help you to get hold of suitable publications

- *other publications*

  section on "Parent Teachers' and Parents' Associations" in *The Law of the School.*

Periodicals and other publications of general interest to parents:

ACE Bulletin (every two months), Advisory Centre for Education. Contains news, comment and advice and a digest of recent reports to do with education and of concern to parents, mainly applying to England and Wales, but with some Scottish items.

British Education Index, The British Library, Bibliographic Services Division, annual edition. Comprehensive annual listing of all published articles of educational interest in over 300 English-language periodicals in alphabetical order of topics.

Childright (ten times a year), Children's Legal Centre.

Dictionary of Education by Derek Rowntree, Harper and Row, 1981. Thousands of educational terms defined.

Education (weekly), Longman.

Education A-Z: where to look things up compiled by Elizabeth Wallis, Advisory Centre for Education, current edition. Quick access to relevant addresses, publications, and terminology on a large number of educational topics, listed alphabetically.

Education Year Book, Longman, annual edition. Comprehensive UK listing of all education authorities, secondary schools, special schools, colleges, universities, careers centres and specialist educational bodies.

EPA INFO — Bulletin of the European Parents' Association, c/o Youth Exchange System, 51 Rue de la Concorde, B-1050, Brussels, Belgium.

History of Scottish Education by James Scotland, University of London Press, 1979 (2 vols).

International Encyclopaedia of Education, ed. Torsten Husen and T. Neville Postlethwaite, Pergamon, 1985 (10 vols). Brings together the latest scholarship through 1,448 articles on educational topics, in alphabetical order.

Parents and Schools (three times a year), Campaign for the Advancement of State Education.

Primary Education Directory (annually), School Government Publishing Co Ltd. Lists name, address and headteacher of every primary school in the UK.

School Governor (quarterly), 73 All Saints Road, Kings Heath, Birmingham B14 7LN.

SCOLAG (monthly), Scottish Legal Action Group.

The Scottish Child (four times a year), Scottish Child Publications, 17 Napier Road, Edinburgh EH10 5AZ.

Scots Law Times (weekly), W. Green & Co. Includes reports on selected sheriff court cases.

Scottish Educational Review (twice yearly), Scottish Academic Press. Articles on research and policy issues in Scottish education.

Secrets, Campaign for Freedom of Information.

SPTC Newspaper, Scottish Parent Teacher Council.

Statistical Bulletin, Scottish Education Department, obtainable from Room 2/65, Scottish Office Library. Periodical publication covering several different educational topics.

Statistical Bulletin, Department of Education and Science, Statistics Branch.

The Times Educational Supplement (weekly), and*The Times Educational Supplement Scotland* (weekly).
Education pages of *The Guardian* (Tuesday), *The Independent* (Thursday),*The Scotsman* (Tuesday) and *Glasgow Herald* (Thursday).

You and Your Rights: an A-Z guide to the law in Scotland, Readers' Digest Association Ltd., 1984.

Background reading

Advisory Centre for Education's handbooks and information sheets on education law, particularly *Guide to Education Law, Special Education Handbook* and *Summary of the Education (No. 2) Act 1986*.

John Bastiani (ed) *Parents and Teachers: perspectives on home-school relations*, NFER, Nelson, 1987.

John Bastiani, *Your Home-School Links*, New Education Press, 1986. A practical guide for parents and teachers.

Consultative Committee on the Curriculum, *Home School Community Relations, Meeting Points* and *Starting Points* (1985) CCC reports and discussion papers on home-school relations.

Consumers' Association, *Children, Parents and the Law*, 1985 (includes coverage of Scotland).

Educational Publishers' Council, *Guide to Schoolbook Spending*.

European Parents' Association, *Parental Access to School Records*, EPA, 1988; *Homework in Europe*, EPA 1988.

Lucy Hodges, *Out into the Open: the school records debate*, Readers' and Writers' Co-operative, 1982.

Daphne Johnson and Elizabeth Ronson, *Family and School*, Croom Helm, 1983. Study of home-school relations in the secondary school years.

Alastair Macbeth, *The Child Between: a report on school-family relations in the countries of the European Community*, Commission of the European Communities, Brussels, 1984.

Alastair Macbeth, *Involving Parents*, Heinemann, 1988.

J. McBeath et al, *Home from School: report of the Guidance and Home Research Project*, Jordanhill College of Education, Glasgow, 1986.

National Children's Bureau, *Parental Involvement in Schooling: a review of research*. Highlight No. 57, 1983.

National Consumer Council, *The Missing Links between Home and School: a consumer view*, 1986.

National Consumer Council, *Consuming Secrets,*Burnett Books, 1982 (see Chapter 5 on Education).

Geoffrey Naylor, Laurie Green and John Allard, *School Reports and Parents' Evenings*, Home and School Council, 1986.

Sarah Sandow, David Stafford and Penny Stafford, *An Agreed Understanding? Parent-professional communication and the 1981 Education Act*, NFER-Nelson, 1987.

Scottish Consumer Council, *The Law of the School: a parents' guide to education law in Scotland*, HMSO Books, 1987.

Scottish Education Department, free booklets on *Choosing a School, The Assisted Places Scheme,* and *Special Educational Needs* (also obtainable from Citizens' Advice Bureaux and other local advice centres, from public libraries or education offices).

Scottish Information Office, free factsheets on *Universities in Scotland* (no. 15), *The Scottish Office* (no. 20), *Local Government in Scotland* (no. 28), *The 16+ Development Programme* (no. 31), and *Setting New Standards for All Scottish Pupils*.

Scottish Parent Teacher Council, *Why have a PTA? Setting up a PTA, Ideas for an Active PTA* and other publications. The SPTC also publishes a regular newsletter.

Barry Taylor, *A Parent's Guide to Education*, Consumers' Association, 1983 (mostly about the education system of England and Wales, but of general interest to parents in Scotland as well).

Sheila Wolfendale, *Parental Participation in Children's Development and Education,* Gordon and Briach, 1983.

Welsh Consumer Council, *Parent and School: a report for discussion between parents and secondary schools in Wales, 1984.*

Official and professional educational organisations

Assistant Masters and Mistresses Association (AMMA)
7 Northumberland Street,
London WC2N 5DA (01 930 6441).

Association of County Councils (ACC)
Eaton House,
66a Eaton Square,
London SW1W 9BH (01 235 1200).

Association of Directors of Education Scotland
c/o Director of Education,
Lothian Regional Council,
40 Torphichen Street,
Edinburgh EH3 8JJ (031 229 9166).

Association of Metropolitan Authorities (AMA)
35 Great Smith Street,
London SW1P 3BJ (01 222 8100).

Chartered Institute of Public Finance and Accountancy (CIPFA)
Scottish Branch,
Strathclyde House,
20 India Street,
Glasgow G2 4PF (041 204 2900).

Chartered Institute of Public Finance and Accountancy (CIPFA)
2-3 Robert Street,
London WC2N 6BH (01 930 3456).

Commission for Local Administration in England
21 Queen Anne's Gate,
London SW1H 9BU (01 222 5622).

Commission for Local Administration in Wales
Derwen House,
Court Road,
Bridgend,
Mid Glamorgan CF31 1BN (0656 61325).

Commissioner for Local Administration in Scotland (Local Ombudsman)
5 Shandwick Place,
Edinburgh EH2 4RG (031 229 4472).

Commissioner for Local Authority Accounts in Scotland
18 George Street,
Edinburgh EH2 1QU (031 226 7346).

Convention of Scottish Local Authorities (COSLA)
Rosebery House, 9 Haymarket Terrace,
Edinburgh EH12 5XZ (031 346 1222).

Council for Educational Technology for the United Kingdom
3 Devonshire Street,
London NW1 2BA (01 580 7553/4)

Council of Local Education Authorities (CLEA)
Eaton House,
66a Eaton Square,
London SW1W 9BH (01 235 1200).

Curriculum Council for Wales
Suite 2, Castle Buildings,
Womanby Street,
Cardiff CF1 9SX (0222) 344946

Department of Education and Science (DES)
Elizabeth House,
York Road,
London SE1 7PH (01 934 9000).
   for obtaining publications:
Publications Despatch Centre,
Government Buildings,
Honeypot Lane,
Stanmore,
Middlesex HA7 1AZ.

Educational Institute of Scotland (EIS)
46 Moray Place,
Edinburgh EH3 6BH (031 225 6244).

Educational Publishers Council (EPC)
19 Bedford Square,
London WC1 (01 580 6321).

Houses of Parliament
Westminster,
London SW1 (01 219 3000).

National Association of Headteachers (NAHT)
Holly House,
6 Paddockhall Road,
Haywards Heath,
West Sussex RH16 1RG (0444 416381).

National Association of Schoolmasters/Union of Women Teachers (NAS/UWT)
Hillscourt Education Centre,
Rose Hill,
Rednal,
Birmingham B45 8RS (021 453 7221/4).

National Foundation for Educational Research
The Mere,
Upton Park,
Slough SL1 2DQ (0753 74123).

National Union of Teachers (NUT)
Hamilton House,
Mabledon Place,
London WC1H 9BD (01 388 6191).

Professional Association of Teachers (PAT)
in Scotland:
22 Rutland Street,
Edinburgh EH1 2AN (031 229 7868).
in England and Wales:
99 Friar Gate,
Derby DE1 1EZ (0332 372337).

School Curriculum Development Committee/National Curriculum Council
Newcombe House,
45 Notting Hill Gate,
London W11 3JB (01 229 1234).

Scottish Community Education Council
Atholl House,
2 Canning Street,
Edinburgh EH3 8EG (031 229 2433).

Scottish Consultative Council on the Curriculum (publications)
Scottish Curriculum Development Service,
Gardyne Road,
Dundee DD5 1NY (0382 455053)

Scottish Council for Educational Technology (SCET)
74 Victoria Crescent Road,
Glasgow G12 9JN (041 334 9314).

Scottish Council for Research in Education (SCRE)
Moray House College,
15 St John Street,
Edinburgh EH8 8JR (031 557 2944).

Scottish Educational Data Archive
Centre for Educational Sociology,
University of Edinburgh,
Buccleuch Place,
Edinburgh 8 (031 667 1011).

Scottish Education Department (SED)
New St Andrews House,
Edinburgh EH1 2SX (031 556 8400).
   for obtaining publications:
Room 323, 43 Jeffrey Street, Edinburgh EJ 1DN
   (for Departmental Circulars)
Scottish Office Library, New St Andrew's House
   (for all other departmental publications not available from HMSO).

Scottish Information Office
New St Andrews House,
Edinburgh EH1 3TD (031 244 1111).
   (for free government booklets, leaflets, etc.).

Scottish Secondary Teachers' Association (SSTA)
15 Dundas Street,
Edinburgh EH3 6QG (031 556 5919).

Scottish Vocational Education Council
38 Queen Street,
Glasgow G1 3DY (041 248 7900).

Secondary Examinations Council (SEC)
Newcombe House,
45 Notting Hill Gate,
London W11 3JB (01 229 1234).

Secondary Heads Association (SHA)
130 Regent Road,
Leicester LE1 7PG (0533 471797).

Society of Education Officers (SEO)
21-27 Lambs Conduit Street,
London WC1N 3NJ (01 831 1973).

Undeb Cenedlaethol Athrawon Cymru
(National Association of the Teachers of Wales) (UCAC)
Pen Roc,
Rhodfa'r Mor,
Aberystwyth,
Dyfed SY23 2AZ (0970 615577).

Welsh Joint Education Committee
245 Western Avenue,
Cardiff CF5 2YX (0222 561231).

Welsh Office Education Department
Crown Offices,
Cathays Park,
Cardiff CF1 3NQ (0222 825111).

(For a more comprehensive list of Scottish organisations, see *The Law of the School*)

Action for Governors Information and Training (AGIT)
c/o CEDC,
Briton Road,
Coventry CV2 4LF (0203 440814).

Advisory Centre for Education (ACE)
18 Victoria Park Square,
London E2 9PB (01 980 4596).

Campaign for the Advancement of State Education (CASE)
4 Hill Road, Carshalton Beeches, Surrey (01 669 5929).

Centre for Studies in Integration in Education
4th Floor,
415 Edgeware Road,
London NW2 6NB (01 452 8642).

Children's Legal Centre
20 Compton Terrace,
London N1 2UN (01 359 6251).

Citizens Advice Scotland
26 George Square,
Edinburgh EH8 9LD (031 667 0156/7).

Consumers' Association
14 Buckingham Street,
London WC2N 6DS (01 839 1222).

81 Action
52 Magnaville Road,
Bishops Stortford, Herts (0279 503244)

European Parents' Association
51 Rue de la Concorde,
B-1050 Brussels, Belgium.

Gifted Children's Information Centre
21 Hampton Lane,
Solihull,
West Midlands (021 226 4541).

Home and School Council
81 Rustlings Road,
Sheffield SI1 7AB (0742 662467).

Independent Schools Information Service (Scotland) (ISIS)
for Scotland:
22 Hanover Street,
Edinburgh EH2 2EP (031 225 7202).
for England:
56 Buckingham Gate,
London SW1E 6AG (01 630 8793).

National Association of Citizens Advice Bureaux (NACAB)
Myddleton House,
115-123 Pentonville Road,
London N1 9LZ (01 833 2181).

National Association of Governors and Managers (NAGM)
81 Rustlings Road,
Sheffield SI1 7AB (0742 662467).

National Children's Bureau
8 Wakeley Street,
London EC1V 7QE (01 278 9441).

National Confederation of Parent Teacher Associations (NCPTA)
2 Ebbsfleet Industrial Estate,
Stonebridge Road,
Gravesend,
Kent DA11 9DZ (0474 560618).

National Consumer Council
20 Grosvenor Gardens,
London SW1W 0DH (01 730 3469).

National Council for Civil Liberties (NCCL)
21 Tabard Street,
London SE1 4LA (01 403 3888).

Parent Teacher Association of Wales (PTAW)
Talgoed,
Pen y Lôn,
Mynydd Isa,
Yr Wyddgrug,
Clwyd CH7 6YG (0352 4652).

Right to Comprehensive Education
36 Broxash Road,
London SW11 6AB (01 228 9732).

Scottish Child Law Centre
1 Melrose Street,
Glasgow G4 4BJ (041 332 9305)
Freefone for under 18s — dial 100.

82 Nicolson Street,
Edinburgh EH8 9EW (031 667 0156).

Scottish Consumer Council
314 St Vincent Street,
Glasgow G3 8XW (041 226 5261).

Scottish Council for Civil Liberties
146 Holland Street,
Glasgow G1 4NG (041 332 5960).

Scottish Parent Teacher Council (SPTC)
30 Rutland Square,
Edinburgh (031 229 0031).

Scottish Telephone Referral Advice and Information Network
74 Victoria Crescent Road,
Glasgow G12 9JN (041 357 1774).

Welsh Consumer Council (WCC)
Castle Buildings,
Womanby Street,
Cardiff CF1 2BN (0222 396056).

Note Page numbers prefixed with (S), indicate the information refers only to Scottish law and (E&W) for legislation in England and Wales.

The alphabetical order is letter by letter. Titles and Acts of Parliament are in italics.

(Indexed by Elizabeth Wallis of the Advisory Centre for Education)

Printed in Scotland for HMSO by McQueen Ltd., Galashiels
Dd. 287166 C80 10/88